A McGRAW-HILL NEW BIOLOGY

Scientific Adviser: Dr. Gwynne Vevers

CHIMPANZEES

OTHER BOOKS IN THIS SERIES

A McGRAW-HILL NEW BIOLOGY

Prue Napier

Chimpanzees

Illustrated by Douglas Bowness

McGRAW-HILL BOOK COMPANY

New York   San Francisco

We gratefully acknowledge our debt to the many
workers, particularly Jane van Lawick-Goodall
and Hugo van Lawick, whose research in
Africa has provided us with so much
information about the natural
lives of chimpanzees.
P.N. and D.B.

Library of Congress Cataloging in Publication Data

Napier, Prue H
  Chimpanzees.

  (A McGraw-Hill new biology)
  Includes index.
  SUMMARY: Describes the characteristics and habits
of chimpanzees, including their group society,
communication techniques, and intelligence.
  1. Chimpanzees—Juvenile literature.
[1. Chimpanzees] 1. Bowness, Douglas.
II. Title.
QL737.P96N36   599'.884   75–28009
ISBN 0–07–045870–7 lib. bdg.

CHIMPANZEES
First distribution in the United States of America
by McGraw-Hill Book Company, 1976.
Text © Prue Napier 1974.
Illustrations © Douglas Bowness 1974.
First printed in Great Britain for
The Bodley Head
by William Clowes & Sons Ltd., Beccles
First published 1974

Contents

1
Introducing the chimpanzee

Of all the animals in the world, the chimpanzee is most closely related to man. This may seem rather surprising because at first glance chimpanzees do not look at all like humans. Their shaggy black fur is very different from the smooth skin of the human body. Even the shape of their bodies is different: very long arms, rather short legs and feet like a second pair of hands. But these differences become less striking if we examine them a little more closely and know something about the chimpanzee's natural life.

Look at almost any part of the human body— the back of your hand, for instance. It is covered with tiny hairs that are almost invisible. There are probably as many hairs on the human body as there are on the chimpanzee's, but they are neither so long nor so dark. Look at a chimpanzee's eyes; notice how they look straight back into your own. With its beautifully shaped ears, short rather squashed nose and expressive mouth, it certainly looks much more like a man than any other animal does.

Examine a young chimpanzee's teeth, and you will find that it has the same number of milk teeth as a child—twenty. Later on when it is grown up, it will have thirty-two teeth—exactly the same number as a man. Other similarities include such basic things as its body temperature (taken with a thermometer), its blood pressure, pulse rate and breathing rate.

Then why is it that chimpanzees, who are so closely related to man, *look* so very different?

A long time ago in the forests of Africa there lived a group of animals that were the ancestors of both man and chimpanzees. They are extinct now, of course, but we know quite a lot about them because scientists have taught us how to understand the evidence of their fossil bones.

The extinct ancestor of man and chimpanzees probably looked rather like a monkey.

These creatures left descendants who lived in two very different kinds of habitat, the forest and the open country, which consisted of grasslands and rather sparse woodland thickets. The sort of food to be found in forests is very different from that found in grasslands, so the ape and human ancestors started to grow apart in the things that they ate and the way in which they found their food. Moving about in trees is very different from moving about on the ground. The ape ancestors had to climb, suspend themselves from overhead branches and stretch out to reach the fruit and nuts on which they fed. They needed long arms, long flexible hook-like hands, and feet with a "thumb" rather than a big toe, which could grasp hold of branches.

9

Ground-living creatures like the human ancestors needed compact and skillful hands capable of plucking grass and collecting seeds. They also needed long strong legs, and feet firm enough to support their weight yet supple and springy enough to propel them forward during walking. Evolution, the natural process by which animals change as time goes by, led finally to the development of two distinct kinds of animal—the apes and man—from a single common ancestor. Evolution is a very slow, gradual process. In this case about ten to fifteen million years have passed since the ape and human ancestors separated.

Like all living things, chimpanzees are given a scientific name, *Pan troglodytes*. *Pan* means "god of the woods" and *troglodytes* means "living in caves."

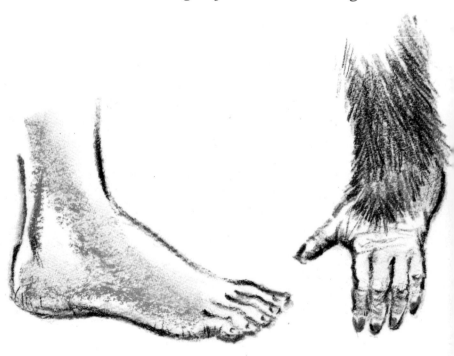

Although chimpanzees may be gods of the woods, they certainly don't live in caves, but we must remember that these names were given them by early zoologists who knew nothing whatsoever about wild chimpanzees.

The common chimpanzee lives in the forests and woodlands of East, Central and West Africa, north of the river Congo. South of the Congo, in the great northward arc of the river, is found the slightly smaller pygmy chimpanzee (*Pan paniscus*, "little god of the woods") about which we know very little as it is seldom seen in zoos and has not yet been studied in the wild.

The pygmy chimpanzee.

2
How chimpanzees live

Chimpanzees are only to be found within the tropics near the Equator. They range from about latitude 10 degrees North to 7 degrees South. Here in the warm tropical rain forests, summer and winter are much the same. Flowers bloom and fruit ripens all around the year, and the trees are always leafy and green.

Monkeys and apes have never acquired the habit of storing food when it is plentiful, to eat later when it is scarce, as squirrels and hamsters do. They have to live where there is an all-year-round supply of fruit and leaves, and this is what the tropical rain forest provides. Chimpanzees also live in woodland-savanna where the seasons are alternately rainy and dry. Instead of raining almost every day as it does in the tropical rain forests, a long rainy season is followed by a long dry season when the thin rather spindly trees shed their scanty leaves. Here the forest is broken up into small patches, in valleys or along river banks, and surrounded by grasslands dotted with clumps of trees. At the end of the dry season there is little food left for the chimpanzees except the nourishing seeds of trees which the Africans call the Muba and Muturu.

Chimpanzees eat mainly plant foods, fruit, particularly figs of many kinds, palm-nuts and leaves. They also eat insects—ants, termites, bees (and honey)—birds and birds' eggs, and occasionally they catch and kill young monkeys, young bushbuck and young bushpig.

Figs and Muba seeds.

Looking for food is the mainspring of a chimpanzee's life and occupies most of the day. Perhaps this is why they look so bored in zoos where they are deprived of this absorbing occupation! Chimpanzees are wonderfully adapted for fruit picking. Their long arms and hook-like hands are ideal for this sort of activity and also provide them with the means of swinging from branch to branch and from tree to tree. This is the special talent of the apes and is called brachiation.

When traveling any distance on the ground, a chimpanzee always walks on all fours. The sole of the foot is placed flat on the ground but the fingers of the hand are bent so that the weight is carried on the backs of the knuckles. As a chimpanzee's arms are slightly longer than its legs, its back slopes from shoulders to hips.

Chimpanzees may occasionally kill other mammals for food but they themselves have few enemies. The leopard is probably the only animal capable of killing an adult chimpanzee but it has never been

known to do so. Chimpanzees seem quite un-
concerned about possible enemies, and they wander
about on the forest floor or in the grasslands, often
quite alone. Sometimes they even move about at
night, particularly under the floodlit brilliance of a
tropical full moon.

But for most chimpanzees, bedtime comes just
before sunset when they each build a sleeping nest
in the trees. Every chimpanzee is an expert at this,
except for the infants who still sleep with their
mothers. In just a few minutes, leafy branches are
bent inwards onto a flat base—a forked branch, for
instance—and roughly woven into a platform. The

leaves make a soft springy bed where the chimpanzee can stretch out and relax. Usually a few adjustments are needed—leaves bunched under the head and uncomfortable twigs snapped off—before the chimpanzee settles down for the night. Nests are built from 15 to 100 feet above the ground and a fresh one is made every night.

Nests are not roofed for protection against rain; the chimpanzee hunches its body and lets the rain roll off its back. Nests are sometimes made during the day in the rainy season when it is too cold and damp to sit on the ground. Chimpanzees never shelter from the rain; they sit in the open, looking miserable, and occasionally shaking themselves to throw off the raindrops clinging to their coats.

3
Chimpanzee society

Chimpanzees live in big communities of about thirty to fifty individuals, but occasionally there may be as many as eighty. There are usually about twice as many grown-up females as males, and twice as many adults as young animals. In a group in West Africa, there were seven adult males and sixteen adult females—that is twenty-three adult animals—and twenty-two young ones (five adolescents, six juveniles and eleven infants), forty-five in all.

Fruit, the main food of chimpanzees, is found on trees that are scattered widely throughout the forest. If fifty chimpanzees all tried to feed from a single tree at the same time, it would not do either the chimps or the tree much good. The chimps would not get enough to eat and the branches of the tree would break under their weight. So the group is usually split up into small units. There may be all-male units of five or six grown-up males; small bands of mothers with their young; and often mixed parties of males and females, adults and young, all traveling together. The unique feature of chimpanzee society is the meeting, mingling and separating of these small units as they roam through the forest in their search for food.

When a band of chimpanzees finds a tree with

plenty of ripe fruit they become wildly excited and bark loudly. This alerts other small bands in the neighborhood who make their way to the spot. After the excitement of meeting is over, they settle down to feed. Later, as each chimpanzee has eaten his fill, they split up, some going in one direction, some in another. Towards sunset, the remainder may nest nearby for the night, returning to the food-tree in the morning.

A chimpanzee group inhabits a part of the forest which is usually called its "home range." This area is their home. They know every tree and bush and pathway through the thick undergrowth. The range has no fixed boundaries and may overlap the home range of a neighboring group.

The home range may be quite small. In a tropical rain forest, where food is always plentiful and the trees are closely packed together, it may be only about two square miles. This is much bigger than it sounds because the forest canopy may rise 150 to 200 feet above the ground and this is all part of the chimpanzees' world.

In woodlands the food sources are scattered and seasonal. In winter chimpanzees congregate in the river valleys where the delicious Ilombo fruits are ripening, while in summer they must migrate, sometimes five or ten miles, to the hills where the Muturu trees can be found. So during a year a woodland-living group may range over 100 square miles.

Ilombo frui

4
The birth of a chimpanzee

Mammals give birth and care for their young in a unique way. A new life begins as a single cell, when the female egg, or ovum, is fertilized inside the female's body by the male sperm. Inside its mother the young mammal, well protected from harm, develops until it is ready to be born. This period of development is called gestation. After birth, the infant sucks milk from its mother's breast until it is able to feed itself.

Chimpanzees are in the adolescent or "growing-up" stage of their lives between seven and thirteen years of age; at this time their bodies are changing to prepare them for mating and giving birth. Sperms develop in the testes of the male and are stored there, ready for mating. These fragile cells are tiny, far too small to be seen except under a microscope, and they cannot survive for long outside the body.

In the female, eggs develop in the ovaries which lie near tubes leading into the uterus where the baby will develop before birth. By the time the female chimpanzee is about ten years old, a regular sequence of events has developed. Every five weeks or so, a single egg starts to grow in size. After a few days, it bursts out of the ovary and makes its way down the tube towards the uterus. This event—

called ovulation—is marked by the appearance of a large pink swelling on the female's hindquarters which, we think, acts as a signal to the males that she is ready to mate with them. Scent is probably an important signal, too. Male chimpanzees often examine and sniff at the swelling before proceeding to mate.

Mating may take place on the ground or high in the trees. The female usually crouches with arms and legs bent while the male approaches from be-

hind. To transfer the fragile sperms safely to the female, the penis is pushed into the vagina which leads to the uterus. This action causes certain muscles to contract, propelling the sperms from the testes into the vagina. Millions of sperms are

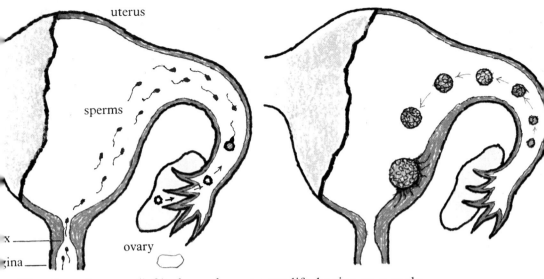

The first diagram (left) shows how a new life begins as a male sperm fertilizes the female egg, forming a single cell. The second diagram (right) shows how the cell grows by dividing into two cells, then four, then eight and so on.

deposited at each mating. Each sperm is able to move by lashing with its powerful tail. In this way they "swim" up into the uterus through a narrow opening called the cervix. Some reach the egg which is fertilized when one of the sperms succeeds in penetrating its outer wall. Now gestation begins, and this lasts about eight months.

First of all the fertilized egg attaches itself firmly to the wall of the uterus, where a system of blood vessels develops, called the placenta. Through this, nourishment is carried from the mother to the growing chimpanzee by a lifeline—the umbilical cord—leading to its umbilicus, or navel. A watery fluid fills the uterus which protects the baby from harm, yet allows it plenty of room to move its limbs. Naturally the mother's abdomen becomes very swollen as gestation progresses. Her breasts swell

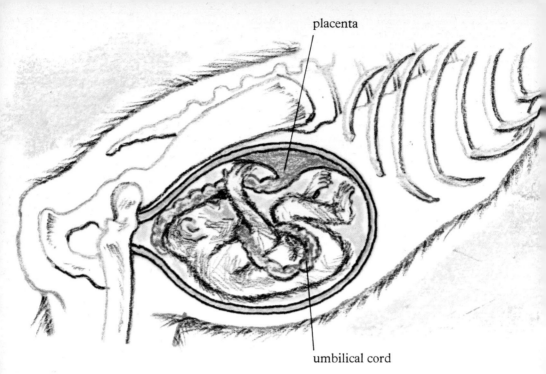

placenta

umbilical cord

too as the milk glands develop in readiness for feeding the baby.

When the time comes for the birth, the female leaves the group to have the baby quietly on her own. Births are fairly quick and easy as the baby is small, about twelve inches from head to foot and weighing only about four pounds. The cervix expands to allow the baby to pass through, and the powerful muscles of the uterus push it out into the world, followed a few minutes later by the placenta, or afterbirth, to which the baby is still attached.

At birth a chimpanzee is weak and helpless. Rather like a human baby, it can do nothing for itself and depends entirely on its mother. An experienced mother, who has had a baby before, immediately picks it up and licks it, cleaning the fluid from its face and rather sparse fur. She bites

24

off the umbilical cord a few inches from the navel (the stump will soon dry up and drop off) and she may eat the placenta or a part of it. But how does an inexperienced mother manage? She is probably helped by having watched other mothers in the group bringing up their babies.

When moving about with a newborn infant, mothers have to take short steps, keeping their legs bent to help support the baby. But it is slow and tiring and they often stop to rest. The baby needs constant cradling. Held in its mother's arms, it can easily reach her nipples. To begin with, it feeds for a few minutes at a time, at least once every hour.

5
Growing up

A chimpanzee mother brings up her baby without any help, except perhaps from her own older off-spring, who are often more of a nuisance than a help because they are so fascinated by the new baby that they are always trying to handle and play with it. Males are not directly involved; there are no "fathers" in chimpanzee society. All adult males are interested in all newborn infants and, when a mother first returns to the group after giving birth, the males examine the baby intently. A baby chimp grows up in a sociable and friendly atmosphere and, naturally, it becomes sociable and friendly too.

At first the baby can do little but feed from its mother's breast and cling to her fur with its hands and feet, but within a month it begins to take notice of its surroundings and, by two months, it is making feeble attempts to clutch at nearby leaves and twigs.

By three months the infant chimp has grown an appealing white tail-tuft and soon, with a little help, it can stand upright on two feet and cling unaided beneath its mother as she walks on all fours. About this time its first teeth are cut—the two lower front ones followed by the two upper front ones—the same order in which our first teeth appear.

/Chimpanzee upbringing seems to be based on tolerance and persuasion rather than on discipline./ When a baby tries to crawl away from its mother, she reaches out and pulls it back firmly but kindly, and then distracts it by playing with it or tickling it. Not until about four or five months is it allowed to leave its mother's arms for the first time, walking rather shakily on all fours or climbing a small sapling. It quickly becomes much more active and soon learns to scramble up on its mother's back where, from now on, she usually carries it. She may even allow it to ride on the back of an older child. At this age the infant takes its first solid food and, by the time it is about a year old, it has cut its full set of twenty baby teeth.

At about a year the young chimpanzee begins to have a life of its own. Its first social contact, apart from its mother, is in playing with other infants. As soon as it is able to climb safely, it spends most of its time playing. Chimpanzees will play by themselves if no one else is available, jumping onto a springy branch again and again. Mostly they play with animals of their own age, chasing and wrestling, poking at each other with sticks, and gamboling about in the most perfect "adventure playground" of all, the forest. Without knowing it, they are developing their bodies, and learning about each other and the world they live in.

Gradually the young chimpanzee learns to find its own food and by about four years old it is weaned. It stops suckling and sleeps apart from its mother who may, by now, have a new baby to care for. Between four and seven years, in the juvenile stage of life, it continues to travel about with its mother but she no longer carries it on her back. During this time the white tail-tuft of babyhood gradually disappears. At about five years of age the first milk teeth are shed and the grown-up teeth take their place.

From seven to thirteen years, in the "growing-up" or adolescent stage, a chimpanzee develops from a child into a fully mature animal. The last permanent teeth—the "wisdom teeth"—are cut at about ten years of age. The female chimpanzee is fully grown at about ten to twelve years when she gives birth to her first baby, but a male is not fully mature until about thirteen years of age. At that stage he may reach about 4 feet to 4 feet 6 inches in height when standing upright and weigh about 120 pounds, while the female is a little smaller.

Chimpanzees may live as long as forty or fifty years. As they get older their faces darken, sometimes becoming completely black, and in old age the hair of the back becomes thin and brownish in color. Bald heads and grey beards are often seen in young adults and so are not necessarily signs of old age.

6
Learning to live in the group

As a chimpanzee grows up, it faces many problems and experiences many rebuffs. It has to learn to fit into a big community and behave suitably to everyone, from the oldest and most respected male to the youngest baby.

Every member of a chimpanzee group has its own distinct rank or status, depending on its age and sex. The big powerful adult males have high status while the smaller females rank lower. If a male walks along a branch where a female is sitting, she will get up to let him pass. But status does not depend on size and strength alone; for instance, infants with white tail-tufts rank highest of all. They are protected by their mothers and treated kindly by everyone. But as the white tail-tuft of babyhood gradually disappears, they lose this privileged status and may be threatened or attacked if they approach an adult. Gradually they learn the rules of chimpanzee society: to keep away from adults particularly when they are feeding, to get out of the way when an adult male is "charging," and to make the correct submissive gestures such as crouching or turning the rump towards an aggressive adult. They learn how to become part of a peaceable and well organized society.

30

One of the times when the young can mix freely with adults is during grooming parties. Grooming consists of examining the fur and skin carefully, and picking off bits of dirt and dry skin with the fingers or lips. A chimpanzee can groom itself on the chest and thighs but for the awkward places—the shoulders and back—it needs a partner. Standing or sitting in front of its chosen partner, it presents a part of its body. Usually the partner responds by grooming it for a few minutes and then asks to be groomed in return. This may go on for hours. Other chimpanzees join the party until as many as ten animals are quietly and peacefully sitting together, grooming away. Young low-ranking chimpanzees groom high-ranking males whom otherwise they would be rather nervous of approaching. Grooming is useful in keeping the fur clean and comfortable, but it also functions as a way of saying "Let's be friends!"

At the center of the group's social life are the adult males. They lead the group, select food-trees and nesting sites, take the initiative in a disturbing or dangerous situation and keep the peace within the group. But leaders are not always male. When a group breaks up into small bands, a female may find herself in the position of leader.

A female exerts her main influence on her own children. A mother and her sons and daughters often meet for family grooming parties, and this strong family link lasts at least until the offspring are fully grown, perhaps even longer. In chimpanzee society, mother *does* know best and a baby chimp learns this lesson early and permanently.

7
How chimpanzees communicate

Chimpanzees are extremely sociable animals. They can communicate their feelings to each other by the expression on their faces, by gestures and by calls.

One of the most exciting calls to be heard in chimpanzee country is the loud long-drawn-out "wraaah" bark of alarm which is given when chimpanzees see something that disturbs them. At close quarters, expression and gesture are combined with calls to show exactly how a chimpanzee is feeling and how it is going to react.

For instance, an adult male feels protective towards an infant who approaches him. His face and body are relaxed as he embraces or pats it, and he may grunt very softly. His whole attitude indicates that he is kindly disposed. But towards another adult male, he may feel aggressive and express this mood by barking and waving his arms. The other male may react to these signals in a number of ways; he may show aggressiveness too, or he may crouch submissively, or he may even run away.

When a chimpanzee is in a state of great excitement, the long hair of its shoulders and arms stands on end, making it look much more intimidating.

Chimpanzees have very expressive faces. Here are some of the more common expressions :

The Play Face. During rather quiet play the lower lip is drawn back, showing the lower teeth.

As the game gets rougher, the upper teeth may also show. Play is sometimes accompanied by soft panting grunts—chimpanzee "laughter."

The Hoot Face is made while giving "pant-hoots," often used when communicating with other chimpanzees in the distance. Push your lips forward as far as you can, to form a trumpet, and breathe in and out rapidly, making a "hoo-ing" noise. If you want to be heard on the other side of the valley, open your mouth wider so that the "hoo" becomes more of a "haaah" noise.

The Grin Face means something rather different from the human smile or grin. It expresses fear. There are several shades of grin face. In alarm, the lips are drawn back, showing the closed teeth but, when badly frightened, the chimpanzee opens its mouth wide, baring teeth and gums. The accompanying calls range from squeaks to loud rasping screams.

The Pout Face, with the lips pushed forward, is accompanied by soft "hoo" calls or whimpers and is often seen in infants when they cannot get their own way.

The Glare. Silently, with lips compressed, a male chimpanzee stares at another. This is an aggressive look, as it is in humans, and is often followed by an attack.

The meaning of hand gestures is often quite obvious. With a begging gesture, palm upwards, and a "hoo" whimper, a chimpanzee begs for a special piece of food. When a female nervously approaches a strange group, she holds out her hand to a big male who touches it for a moment. When two females hear an unusual noise, one puts her arm around the other. Embracing, hugging or even just touching one another seem to have a calming effect on chimpanzees that are alarmed or anxious.

Sometimes an adult male seems to "lose his temper" for no apparent reason. Slowly the chimp's hair begins to stand on end. He glares, hunches his shoulders and sways from side to side. Then with a scream he suddenly explodes into action. He shakes a tree, then breaks off a big branch and charges, dragging it after him as easily as if it were a hockey-stick. He slaps the ground with his hands, then picks up a stone and throws it. He drums on a tree-trunk with his feet, the two feet pounding the tree one after another with a deafening double-beat. Sometimes he finishes the "charging display" by rushing up a tree and leaping down again with much crashing of branches. Occasionally he may attack another chimpanzee, hurling it to the ground and jumping on it. Then—suddenly—it all calms down. The forest is silent. The episode is over.

Usually only adult males display in this way and the habit seems to be infectious. When two familiar groups meet, there is a joyous reunion which looks like a battle but is really a meeting of old friends. Loud screams, roars and drummings echo through the forest, sometimes for hours on end.

8
Chimpanzee intelligence

How intelligent are chimpanzees? We do not know. We tend to judge intelligence from our own point of view, and when a chimpanzee behaves like a human, we automatically say to ourselves, "How very clever!" This is not very intelligent on our part, for what we do know is that chimpanzee intelligence is ideally adapted to chimpanzee life, which is not always easy. Chimpanzees keep themselves well-fed and reasonably comfortable all around the year, in all weathers. Imagine what it would be like camping out in the wild, with no tent, no clothes, no fire, and only the food you could gather to keep alive! It's a tough life, but chimpanzees seem to thrive on it.

New scientific studies of chimpanzees in the wild have shown that they have a much wider range of activities than was thought. For instance, those living in woodland-savanna very occasionally hunt and kill for food. Hunting usually seems to happen on the spur of the moment. If a young baboon strays away from its troop near a group of chimpanzees, it may be grabbed and killed by one of them. The carcass is dragged up a tree, and the others crowd around, begging for a share of the meat. Even the largest and strongest wait patiently

for a handout. Meat is always eaten slowly. A few leaves are eaten with each mouthful which is chewed very thoroughly.

Chimpanzees make use of many objects in their daily lives. I have already described how they weave the leafy branches of trees into sleeping nests. When they feel themselves threatened by a group of baboons, chimpanzees will often attack by hurling sticks or stones at the intruders. Their aim is not very good but the flailing arms and blood-curdling screams which accompany the attack are enough to scare the baboons away.

Chimpanzees explore holes in trees with a stick, sniffing at the end to find out what is inside. They have also been seen to use sticks or stems to "fish" for termites. They carefully insert a long piece of stick into a hole in the termites' nest. When this is gently withdrawn, it is covered with clinging termites which the chimpanzees pick off with their lips. In order to make a "fishing-rod," a chimpanzee selects a slender stem and removes all projecting leaves and twigs, making it smooth and straight. When this was first observed a few years ago, scientists were very astonished because it had always been thought that only humans could make tools.

Chimpanzees are individuals, each with its own personality and talents. If one chimpanzee has a new idea—making its nest in a different kind of tree, for instance—the "craze" will spread by imitation to the rest of the group. Perhaps this is how termite-fishing started.

Many of our ideas about chimpanzees have had to be changed as we have come to know more about them. One particularly intriguing aspect of chimpanzee intelligence is still unsolved. Can chimpanzees be taught to talk? An early attempt to train a chimpanzee to speak was a failure; after six years it could only manage four badly pronounced words. Apparently chimpanzees do not have the same kind of speech mechanism as humans.

Recently two chimpanzees have been taught to communicate with humans by using symbols and

signs instead of spoken words. Sarah, a six year old female, was taught to use colored plastic symbols which could be stuck on a magnetic board. Beginning with apple, orange and banana (which could be given to her as a reward for getting them right!) she learned, not *words*, but *symbols* for many objects, actions and ideas. A blue triangle stood for "apple," a red square for "banana," and so on. Sarah learned to answer questions by "reading" the symbols placed on the board and "writing" the answers. Sarah reads and writes vertically, as the picture shows. It reads, "Sarah take red apple" and I expect that's exactly what Sarah did!

Another unspoken language known as ASL, the American Sign Language which is used by deaf people in North America, was taught to Washoe, a young female chimpanzee. From the time when she was still a baby, about a year old, she learned, by imitation and encouragement, signs for many everyday things and actions such as "more," "dog," "food," "open," "hurry," "toothbrush," and so on. "Come," or "give-me," is a beckoning movement of the hand, palm upwards, very like the begging gesture of wild chimpanzees. When Washoe wants a drink, she clenches her fist and touches her mouth with her extended thumb. Soon she was stringing two or three signs together, like "listen dog" when she heard a dog bark. It is interesting that deaf people can understand what Washoe is "saying," even though she "speaks" with a strong chimpanzee accent.

These two chimpanzees, Washoe and Sarah, have surprised scientists by their ability to learn and understand things which seem to go far beyond what they need in their natural lives.

Chimpanzees' intelligence must be judged by its results, by how well it works in their daily lives. As we know, chimpanzees sometimes share food with one another. A male chimpanzee with some desirable piece of food, like a carcass of freshly-killed meat, is always approached by other chimpanzees, begging for a share. They are very persistent, holding out their hands in a begging gesture and giving soft whimpers. At first the male may ignore their pleas, but soon he responds by tearing off pieces and handing them out. Females and infants may even be allowed to eat from the carcass itself at the same time as the male.

This behavior—which we might call "unselfish" behavior—is valuable because it means that nourishing food is shared with every member of the group, above all with its weakest members, the females and infants. This is good for the group as a whole, particularly when food is scarce. A group that shares its food in this way is likely to be more successful—larger in numbers, stronger and healthier—than one that does not. Maybe this is how food-sharing became part of the chimpanzees' way of life. Perhaps too it was in this sort of way that "unselfish" behavior became part of human societies—for the simple reason that it works.

Index